THE KINSMAN'S PROMISE

Discovering God's Plan for Redemption

Becoming the Person God Created You to Be

Two Complete Studies in One Workbook

By

Melinda Mitchell Newman

STUDY ONE: From Famine to Favor (6 Sessions)

STUDY TWO: From Risk to Redemption (7 Sessions)

The Kinsman's Promise: Discovering God's Plan for Redemption

DEDICATION

For every person who has ever felt stuck, bitter, confused,
or dis-appointed from their destiny.

There is a path forward. His chesed has not stopped.

TABLE OF CONTENTS

HOW TO USE THIS STUDY

Welcome to The Kinsman's Promise. This workbook is designed to help you become the person God created you to be—regardless of where you've been or what detours you've taken.

This workbook can be used as a standalone Bible study or as a companion to the memoir ***Modern Day Ruth: One Widow's Journey from Murder to Destiny Through Forgiveness and Faith***. Whether you're studying on your own, with a small group, or reading alongside the book, each session stands complete with its own teaching, word studies, and application.

The King James Version (KJV) is used in this study, but you are encouraged to use your preferred translation.

TWO COMPLETE STUDIES IN ONE
• STUDY ONE: From Famine to Favor (6 sessions) — Letting go of what holds you back
• STUDY TWO: From Risk to Redemption (7 sessions) — Stepping into your destiny

Churches/Bible Study groups can complete one study per semester or all 13 sessions consecutively.

SESSION FORMAT
Each session (60-90 minutes) includes:
Opening Prayer
Icebreaker
Scripture Reading
Hebrew/Greek Word Study
Teaching Section
Key Themes
Discussion Questions
Personal Reflection
Application Challenge
Closing Prayer
Memory Verse

INTRODUCTION: THE DANGEROUS PRAYER

In September 2001, I sat in my living room studying Ruth. Life was good—beautiful home, healthy boys, a husband I adored. But as I studied Ruth 3:11, I felt convicted: would 'virtuous' describe my character?

I hit the floor crying and prayed: 'God, help me become a modern-day Ruth.'

Four years later, on June 26, 2005, that prayer was answered in a way I never could have imagined.

Someone broke into our home. My husband Tim died protecting our son and our family. I became a widow at 36.

From June 2005 to June 2006, I attended seven funerals. I cried out, 'Lord, show me what You're doing!'

His answer came from John 13:7: 'What I am doing you do not understand now, but afterward you will understand.'

This study will challenge you to confront disobedience, release bitterness, choose forgiveness, and step into your destiny. Are you ready?

— Melinda Mitchell Newman

STUDY ONE

FROM FAMINE TO FAVOR

Six Sessions on Letting Go of What Holds You Back

SESSION ONE

WHEN EVERYONE DOES WHAT'S RIGHT IN THEIR OWN EYES

Obedience vs. Disobedience

Ruth 1:1-5

OPENING PRAYER

Begin with prayer, asking God to open your heart to His Word.

ICEBREAKER

"Have you ever had a plan that didn't happen at all like you planned?"

____

____

____

WORD STUDY

YASHAR (יָשָׁר)

H3477 yah-SHAR

Meaning: straight, upright, pleasing, right

When everyone does what is *'yashar'* in their own eyes without God's standard, the result is chaos. Elimelech's disobedience led to death and devastation.

TEACHING: Understanding the Context

The book of Ruth opens with one of the most chilling phrases in Scripture: "In those days there was no king in Israel." This isn't just historical context—it's spiritual diagnosis. When there's no king, everyone becomes their own authority. Elimelech's name means "my God is King," yet his actions told a different story. When famine came to Bethlehem—the "house of bread"—he didn't seek God's direction. He made a logical decision based on circumstances rather than covenant.

Here's what we miss: Moab wasn't just another country. It was the nation born from Lot's incestuous relationship with his daughter. It was the place where Balak hired Balaam to curse Israel. Deuteronomy 23:3-6 prohibited Moabites from entering the assembly of the Lord for ten generations. (Note: Some scholars observe that the Hebrew uses masculine language, which may explain how Ruth—a woman— could be accepted into Israel's covenant community.) Elimelech didn't just move his family to another town—he took them to the one place God had specifically forbidden.

The consequences were devastating. Within ten years, Elimelech was dead. Both sons married Moabite women—something an Israelite father would never have permitted in Bethlehem. Then both sons died, leaving three widows with no covering, no provision, and no future. One man's "reasonable" disobedience cost his entire family everything. This is why *yashar* matters. When we do what seems right in our own eyes instead of submitting to God's standard, the people we love pay the price.

Consider the names in this story—they reveal the tragedy before it unfolds. Elimelech means "my God is King," yet he acted as his own king. Naomi means "pleasant," but she would later beg to be called Mara—"bitter." Most haunting are the sons: Mahlon means "sickly" and Chilion means "failing" or "wasting away." What parents name their children Sickly and Failing? Perhaps these names reflected physical conditions at birth, or perhaps they were prophetic markers of what disobedience would produce.

The word "sojourn" in Ruth 1:1 is the Hebrew word *gur*, meaning to dwell temporarily as a stranger. Elimelech's plan was never to stay permanently—just survive the famine and return. But notice verse 2: "they continued there." Temporary became permanent. This is one of the enemy's most effective strategies: he rarely invites us to abandon God completely. Instead, he suggests a brief detour, a temporary compromise, a short stay in Moab. Ten years later, we're still there, wondering how we drifted so far from where we started.

Why did God allow famine in Bethlehem—the "House of Bread"? Deuteronomy 11:13-17 explains the connection between Israel's obedience and their harvests. When God's people turned to idolatry, He withheld rain. The famine wasn't random—it was discipline designed to turn hearts back to Him. Elimelech's solution was to escape the consequences rather than address the cause. He ran from the very discipline meant to restore him. How often do we do the same? Instead of asking what God might be teaching us through difficulty, we look for the nearest exit to Moab.

KEY THEMES
- Obedience to God vs. doing what seems right to us
- Consequences of disobedience affect those we love
- Spiritual drift happens gradually
- God is King whether we acknowledge it or not

DISCUSSION QUESTIONS

1. Where might your actions contradict what you claim to believe?

2. What 'Moab' have you run to when life got hard?

3. How does our culture encourage doing what's 'right in our own eyes'?

4. Who is affected by your choices?

5. What does it look like to have God as King over every area?

PERSONAL REFLECTION

• *Is there an area where I'm doing what seems right to ME rather than seeking God?*

• *Where have I drifted spiritually?*

• *What would change if I truly let God be King?*

____

____

____

APPLICATION CHALLENGE

This week: Identify ONE area of disobedience. Find a scripture that speaks to it. Take ONE step of obedience this week.

____

____

____

____

CLOSING PRAYER

"Lord, reveal where I've been my own king. Show me where I've drifted. Help me trust You. Amen."

MEMORY VERSE

"In those days there was no king in Israel: every man did that which was right in his own eyes. — Judges 21:25"

NOTES

SESSION TWO

WHEN GOD PURSUES YOU

He Initiates Even When We've Wandered

Ruth 1:6-7

OPENING PRAYER

Begin with prayer, asking God to open your heart to His Word.

ICEBREAKER

"Share a time when news changed everything—news that made you realize things could be different."

____

____

____

WORD STUDY

PAQAD (פָּקַד)

H6485 pah-KAHD

Meaning: to visit, attend to, care for

When God 'visits' His people, He takes intentional action. God's pursuit reaches us even in our wandering.

TEACHING: The God Who Pursues

Naomi had been in Moab for at least ten years when she heard the news: "The LORD had visited His people in giving them bread." Notice where she heard this—still in Moab. Still in the wrong place. Still in the land of her disobedience. Yet God's pursuit reached her there.

The Hebrew word *paqad* carries profound meaning. When God "visits," He doesn't just stop by—He takes intentional action on behalf of His people. This same word describes God "visiting" Sarah to give her Isaac, God "visiting" Israel in Egypt before the Exodus, and God "visiting" Hannah to give her Samuel. A divine visitation always precedes divine deliverance.

But here's what moves me: God was preparing provision in Bethlehem while Naomi was still sitting in Moab. Before she took one step toward home, the fields were already producing grain. Before she made one decision to return, God had already ended the famine. This is the nature of our God—He prepares before we're ready, provides before we ask, and pursues before we turn. The question isn't whether God is pursuing you. The question is whether you'll respond to what you've heard.

Notice the sequence in Ruth 1:6: "She had heard... that the LORD had visited his people in giving them bread." Naomi heard. Despite ten years in Moab, despite burying her husband and both sons, despite having every reason to stop listening for news from home—she was still paying attention to what God was doing among His people. She hadn't completely disconnected. This is crucial: even in our wandering, even in our Moab seasons, we must keep one ear tuned to what God is doing. The moment we stop listening is the moment we miss our invitation home.

The phrase "giving them bread" is deeply significant. Bethlehem literally means "House of Bread." When Elimelech left, there was famine in the House of Bread—an impossible contradiction that revealed Israel's spiritual condition. Now God was restoring bread to the place named for bread. He was making Bethlehem what it was always meant to be. This is what God does when His people return to Him: He restores things to their intended purpose. He makes the House of Bread full of bread again. He makes bitter Naomi pleasant again. He takes what famine and death have emptied and fills it with life.

Verse 7 says Naomi "went forth out of the place where she was." She arose. She took action. Hearing wasn't enough—she had to respond. The Hebrew word for "arose" (*qum*) implies rising from a position of sitting or lying down, moving from passivity to activity. It's the same word used when God tells Abraham to "arise and walk through the land" (Genesis 13:17). God's visitation requires our participation. He provides the bread, but we must make the journey back to where the bread is. He opens the door, but we must walk through it.

KEY THEMES

- God initiates restoration
- His pursuit reaches us even when we've wandered
- News of provision can reach us in our 'Moab'
- God prepares before we're ready to return

DISCUSSION QUESTIONS

1. What does it mean that God 'visits' His people?

____

____

____

2. Naomi was in Moab for at least 10 years. What does it tell us that God was still pursuing her?

____

____

____

3. Where might God be preparing provision you can't see?

____

____

____

4. Why do some respond to God's provision while others stay where they are?

____

____

____

PERSONAL REFLECTION

• *How has God been pursuing me even when I wasn't pursuing Him?*

____

____

____

• *What 'news' has God sent that I haven't responded to?*

____

____

____

• *Am I still sitting in my Moab?*

____

____

____

APPLICATION CHALLENGE

This week: Look for evidence of God 'visiting' you this week—in Scripture, through others, in circumstances.

CLOSING PRAYER

"Lord, thank You for pursuing me. Open my eyes to see how You're visiting me right now. Amen."

MEMORY VERSE

"...she had heard how the LORD had visited his people in giving them bread. — Ruth 1:6"

NOTES

<h1 style="text-align:center">SESSION THREE</h1>

<h1 style="text-align:center">THE CROSSROADS OF FAITH</h1>

Choosing Obedience Over Comfort

Ruth 1:7-18

OPENING PRAYER

Begin with prayer, asking God to open your heart to His Word.

ICEBREAKER

"Describe a crossroads when you had to choose between the comfortable path and the faith path."

____

____

____

WORD STUDY

DABAQ (דָּבַק)

H1692 dah-BAHK

Meaning: to cling, cleave, hold fast

This is the same word for marriage in Genesis 2:24. Ruth chose fierce, covenant commitment. Also: BATACH (H982) means deep confidence in God; GALAL (H1556) means to 'roll' your way onto God.

TEACHING: The Covenant Choice

Three women stood at a crossroads on the road between Moab and Judah. All three had lost husbands. All three faced uncertain futures. But only one made the covenant choice that would change history.

Naomi urged both daughters-in-law to return to Moab—to their mothers' houses, to their gods, to the familiar. Orpah's choice wasn't evil; it was logical. She kissed her mother-in-law, wept, and went back to what she knew. We never hear of Orpah again. Her story ends at the crossroads.

Ruth's response contains some of the most powerful words of commitment in Scripture: "Entreat me not to leave thee." The Hebrew word *dabaq*—to cling, to cleave—is the same word used in Genesis 2:24 for marriage. Ruth wasn't making a casual promise; she was making a covenant. "Thy people shall be my people, and thy God my God." She chose covenant over comfort, faith over familiarity, and an unknown future with God over a predictable future without Him. Every destiny decision requires this same choice: Will you cling to what you know, or will you cleave to the One who knows your future?

Look carefully at Naomi's argument in verses 11-13. She told Ruth there was no logical reason to follow her: no more sons to marry, no security to offer, no future to promise. Naomi was essentially saying, "I have nothing for you." From a purely practical standpoint, she was right. Orpah weighed the options and made the reasonable choice—she went back to what she knew. But Ruth heard something beyond Naomi's words. She saw something in Naomi's God that was worth more than security in Moab. Ruth's choice was based on faith, not logic.

Ruth's declaration in verses 16-17 contains seven commitments—a number representing completeness in Hebrew thought. She committed her location ("where you go"), her dwelling ("where you lodge"), her community ("your people"), her God ("your God"), her death ("where you die"), her burial ("there will I be buried"), and invoked God as witness ("the LORD do so to me"). This wasn't an emotional outburst—it was a complete, covenant commitment covering every aspect of life and death. Ruth held nothing back.

Here's what makes Ruth's choice extraordinary: she had watched Naomi suffer. She knew that following Naomi's God hadn't protected Naomi from losing everything. Yet Ruth still chose Him. This is mature faith—choosing God not because He guarantees comfort, but because He is worthy regardless of circumstances. Ruth didn't choose Naomi's God because life had gone well for Naomi. She chose Him because she recognized something true about His character that transcended her mother-in-law's pain. What do you see in God that would make you choose Him even if following Him cost you everything?

KEY THEMES
- Faith requires choosing obedience over comfort
- Covenant commitment vs. convenient faith
- We don't need to understand to obey
- Trust (*batach*) means confidence in God's character
- Commit (*galal*) means rolling yourself onto God

DISCUSSION QUESTIONS
1. Why did Naomi urge Ruth to go back?

____

____

____

2. What did Ruth have to gain by going to Bethlehem?

____

____

____

3. Ruth chose Naomi's God after watching her suffer. What does this tell us about authentic faith?

____

____

____

4. What 'Moab' might God be asking you to leave?

____

____

____

PERSONAL REFLECTION

• _Do I typically choose comfort or faith at crossroads?_

____

____

____

• _Is there something I'm clinging to that keeps me from following God?_

____

____

____

• _What would my own 'Ruth declaration' be?_

____

____

____

APPLICATION CHALLENGE

This week: Write your own 'Ruth declaration' for your current season. Post it where you'll see it daily.

CLOSING PRAYER

"Lord, give me Ruth's courage to cling to You even when the logical path leads elsewhere. Amen."

MEMORY VERSE

"Trust in the LORD with all your heart, and lean not on your own understanding. — Proverbs 3:5"

NOTES

SESSION FOUR
THE WEIGHT OF BITTERNESS

What Unforgiveness Costs You
Ruth 1:19-22 • Hebrews 12:15

OPENING PRAYER

Begin with prayer, asking God to open your heart to His Word.

ICEBREAKER

"Have you ever felt like your identity no longer fit who you'd become through painful circumstances?"

____

____

____

WORD STUDY

MARA (מְרָא)

H4755 mah-RAH

Meaning: bitter

Naomi wanted to change her name to 'Bitter.' Her honesty is striking—but she was heading toward a permanent identity defined by pain. Bitterness troubles YOU and defiles MANY (Hebrews 12:15). *DIS-APPOINTED FROM YOUR DESTINY: Disappointment can literally 'dis-appoint' you from your appointed destiny. One way to get dis-appointed is through unforgiveness.*

TEACHING: The Weight We Carry

When Naomi arrived in Bethlehem, the whole city stirred. Women who had known her asked, "Is this Naomi?" Her response reveals what ten years of loss had done to her soul: "Call me not Naomi, call me Mara: for the Almighty hath dealt very bitterly with me."

Naomi means "pleasant." Mara means "bitter." She was asking the community to rename her according to her pain. "I went out full, and the LORD hath brought me home again empty." Notice who she blamed—not Elimelech for his disobedience, not circumstances, not the famine. She blamed God directly: "The LORD hath testified against me, and the Almighty hath afflicted me."

Bitterness is what happens when we assign blame for our pain in the wrong direction. It's the choice to see ourselves as victims of God rather than recipients of His redemption. The tragedy is that Naomi couldn't see what was standing right beside her. She said she came home "empty"—but Ruth was right there. God had already provided, but bitterness blinded her to the blessing. This is what unforgiveness does: it makes us unable to receive what God is trying to give us because we're too focused on what we think He took away.

The Hebrew word for bitter, mara, appears throughout Scripture as a warning. The waters at *Marah* were bitter and undrinkable until God healed them (Exodus 15:23-25). Bitterness makes us undrinkable—toxic to ourselves and others. Hebrews 12:15 warns that a "root of bitterness" doesn't just affect us; it "troubles" us and "defiles many." The people around Naomi—including Ruth—would be affected by whether she held onto Mara or returned to Naomi. Your bitterness is never just about you.

Notice Naomi's theology in verse 21: "The LORD hath testified against me, and the Almighty hath afflicted me." She used two names for God here—LORD (Yahweh, the covenant name) and Almighty (*Shaddai*, the all-sufficient one). Even in her bitterness, she acknowledged who God was. But she interpreted her suffering as God being against her rather than for her. This is the danger of pain without perspective: we can know God's names while completely misunderstanding His nature. Naomi saw God as her adversary when He was actually orchestrating her redemption.

There's an important distinction between honest grief and destructive bitterness. Grief says, "This hurts terribly." Bitterness says, "This hurt defines me." Grief processes pain and eventually moves through it. Bitterness builds an identity around pain and refuses to let it go. Naomi's request to change her name reveals she was crossing from grief into identity—she wanted to be known by her pain rather than her original design. God would eventually restore her, but first she had to be willing to release Mara and reclaim Naomi. What name have you been answering to that was never meant to define you?

KEY THEMES
• Bitterness is honest emotion but not meant to be our identity
• Unforgiveness imprisons US, not the offender
• The root of bitterness defiles many
• Unforgiveness can dis-appoint us from our destiny

DISCUSSION QUESTIONS
1. What's the difference between honest grief and destructive bitterness?

____

____

____

2. How do we process anger at God in healthy ways?

____

____

____

3. Who is affected by your unforgiveness besides you?

____

____

____

4. How might unforgiveness be 'dis-appointing' you from your destiny?

____

____

____

PERSONAL REFLECTION

• *Am I holding onto bitterness I've renamed as something acceptable?*

____

____

____

• *Who am I holding hostage by my unforgiveness?*

____

____

____

• *What has unforgiveness cost me?*

____

____

____

APPLICATION CHALLENGE

This week: Complete the Forgiveness Inventory: List names you're holding hostage. Next session we'll talk about HOW to forgive.

____

____

____

____

CLOSING PRAYER

"Lord, show me what unforgiveness is costing me. Prepare my heart for freedom. Amen."

MEMORY VERSE

"Lest any root of bitterness springing up trouble you, and thereby many be defiled. — Hebrews 12:15"

NOTES

SESSION FIVE

THE FREEDOM OF FORGIVENESS

How Forgiveness Unlocks Your Destiny
Genesis 50:15-21 • Colossians 3:13 • Luke 23:34

OPENING PRAYER

Begin with prayer, asking God to open your heart to His Word.

ICEBREAKER

"What's hardest about forgiveness—understanding it, choosing it, or walking it out?"

WORD STUDY

MNAOMAI (μνάομαι)

G3415 MNAH-oh-my

Meaning: to remind, recall, bring up

God is omniscient—He can't forget. Yet He 'remembers our sins no more' (Hebrews 8:12). He CHOOSES not to focus on it, not to bring it up, not to hold it against us.

APHIEMI (ἀφίημι)

G863 af-EE-ay-mee

Meaning: to send away, release, let go, forgive

The New Testament word for forgiveness—an active release, not a passive feeling.

TEACHING: The Path to Freedom

Forgiveness is not a feeling—it's a decision. It's not saying what happened was okay. It's not minimizing your pain or excusing the one who caused it. Forgiveness is releasing your right to revenge and trusting God to be the judge.

Joseph understood this. After everything his brothers did—selling him into slavery, lying to their father, leaving him to suffer in Egypt for years—he said, "Ye thought evil against me; but God meant it unto good." Joseph didn't pretend the evil wasn't evil. He acknowledged what they intended. But he also recognized what God accomplished through it. Forgiveness allowed Joseph to see past his brothers' intentions to God's purposes.

Jesus commanded us to forgive "seventy times seven"—not because the offender deserves it, but because unforgiveness imprisons us. The person who hurt you may never apologize. They may never acknowledge your pain. They may never change. But your freedom doesn't depend on their repentance. Your freedom depends on your obedience. When you forgive, you're not letting them off the hook— you're letting yourself off the hook of bitterness that will poison every relationship and blessing God wants to bring into your life.

The Greek word for forgiveness in the New Testament is *aphiemi*, meaning to send away, release, or let go. It's the same word used when Jesus told the disciples to "let down" their nets (Luke 5:4) and when He "dismissed" the crowds (Matthew 13:36). Forgiveness is an active release—you're choosing to let go of something you have every right to hold. The debt is real. The offense happened. But you're releasing your grip on it, sending it away from you rather than clutching it close.

Consider the word picture in Hebrews 8:12, where God says He will "remember their sins no more." God is omniscient—He literally cannot forget. So what does it mean that He remembers our sins no more? The Hebrew concept behind this is choosing not to bring something up, not to hold it against someone, not to let it define the relationship going forward. This is what we're called to do: not to erase our memory of what happened, but to choose not to weaponize it, not to keep bringing it up, not to let it determine how we treat the person.

Forgiveness is often a process, not a one-time event. You may need to forgive the same person for the same offense repeatedly—not because the first forgiveness didn't "take," but because pain has a way of resurfacing. Each time the memory returns with fresh anger, you have another opportunity to release it again. Jesus told Peter to forgive "seventy times seven"—not because someone will wrong you 490 times, but because true forgiveness sometimes requires choosing release over and over until the grip finally loosens. Every time you're tempted to pick up that offense again, lay it back down.

WHAT FORGIVENESS IS AND ISN'T

FORGIVENESS IS: A choice (not a feeling), releasing the debt, choosing not to bring it up, giving it to God, freedom for YOU

FORGIVENESS IS NOT: Forgetting, excusing, reconciliation, trusting again, a one-time event

"What you focus on, you make room for." — John Paul Jackson

FROM MY STORY

On June 26, 2005, my husband Tim was murdered protecting our son. I had a choice: stay imprisoned by bitterness or walk the hard road of forgiveness. It wasn't instant. It wasn't easy. But forgiveness unlocked my destiny. — Melinda Mitchell Newman

KEY THEMES

- 'Remember no more' means choosing not to bring it up
- Forgiveness is a choice, not a feeling
- What you focus on, you make room for (John Paul Jackson)
- We forgive because we have been forgiven

DISCUSSION QUESTIONS

1. How does understanding that God 'chooses not to bring it up' change your view of forgiveness?

____

____

____

2. Which is harder—forgiving others or forgiving yourself?

____

____

____

3. Joseph saw God's purpose in his suffering. Can you see any in yours?

____

____

____

4. How might unforgiveness be blocking your destiny?

____

____

____

PERSONAL REFLECTION

- *Go back to your Forgiveness Inventory. Are you ready to release any names?*

____

____

____

• *What would life look like without this bitterness?*

____

____

____

APPLICATION CHALLENGE

This week: Every time the offense comes to mind, 'change the channel.' Thank God for His forgiveness. Choose not to rehearse the offense.

____

____

____

____

____

CLOSING PRAYER

"Lord, I choose to forgive _________. I release them from the debt. I give You the right to judge. Amen."

MEMORY VERSE

"Forgiving one another... even as Christ forgave you. — Colossians 3:13"

NOTES

SESSION SIX
TAKING THE FIRST STEP

Obedient Initiative
Ruth 2:1-7

OPENING PRAYER

Begin with prayer, asking God to open your heart to His Word.

ICEBREAKER

"What's hardest about taking action when you're exhausted and uncertain?"

____

____

____

WORD STUDY

LAQAT (לָקַט)

H3950 lah-KAHT

Meaning: to pick up, gather, glean

Ruth didn't wait for provision—she went out looking. Gleaning was humble work, but she took initiative. And 'her hap was to light on' Boaz's field—divine providence disguised as coincidence.

TEACHING: Initiative and Obedience

The Hebrew word *laqat* means to gather, to collect, to pick up what others have left behind. Gleaning was provision of last resort in Israel. Leviticus 19:9-10 and Deuteronomy 24:19-21 commanded landowners to leave the edges of their fields unharvested and not to go back for forgotten sheaves— these were for the poor, the foreigner, the widow, and the orphan. Ruth qualified on multiple counts.

But gleaning was hard, humbling work. It meant following behind the reapers in the hot sun, bending down again and again to pick up scraps others had left behind. Everyone in the field would know Ruth was poor, foreign, and desperate.

But Ruth went anyway. She didn't let pride keep her from provision. She didn't wait for something better. She didn't demand that God provide in a different way. She simply said, "Let me go," and Naomi said, "Go, my daughter." Ruth's willingness to embrace humble provision rather than demand something better positioned her for favor she never could have earned.

Sometimes the breakthrough we're waiting for is waiting for us to take the first step. God guides moving feet. He can't steer a parked car. Ruth's initiative positioned her for the "just so happened" that was about to change everything.

The phrase "her hap was to light on" in Ruth 2:3 is fascinating. The Hebrew suggests something that appears to be chance or accident. From Ruth's perspective, she randomly ended up in Boaz's field. But the narrator wants us to see what Ruth couldn't: there are no accidents in God's economy. What looks like coincidence is actually providence. Ruth made herself available by going to the fields; God directed her steps to the right field. This is how divine guidance often works—we take the step we can see, and God handles the steps we can't.

Notice Ruth asked permission: "Let me now go... and glean." She didn't assume or demand. Even though the Law entitled her to glean, she approached with humility and respect, asking rather than taking. This attitude would catch Boaz's attention later (Ruth 2:7). How we receive provision matters as much as whether we receive it. Ruth's character in the small act of asking permission was building a reputation that would precede her into greater opportunities. What "gleaning" has God put before you that you've dismissed as beneath you? What humble first step are you refusing to take while waiting for God to provide in a different way?

KEY THEMES
• Obedience often requires initiative
• Humble work is honorable work
• Divine providence often looks like coincidence
• Take the first step—God will direct your path

DISCUSSION QUESTIONS
1. Ruth went out looking. What does this teach about faith and action?

____

____

____

2. What 'gleaning' has God asked you to do that felt beneath you?

____

____

____

3. How have you seen God's hand in what looked like coincidence?

____

____

____

4. What first step might God be asking you to take?

____

____

____

PERSONAL REFLECTION

• *Am I waiting for provision or willing to go glean?*

____

____

____

• *What pride keeps me from accepting humble provision?*

____

____

____

• *What first step have I been avoiding?*

____

____

____

APPLICATION CHALLENGE

This week: Identify one action step you've been avoiding. Take that step this week.

____

____

____

____

CLOSING PRAYER

"Lord, give me Ruth's initiative. Lead me to the right fields. Help me see Your hand. Amen."

MEMORY VERSE

"Let me now go to the field, and glean ears of corn. — Ruth 2:2"

NOTES

STUDY ONE CONCLUSION: FINDING FAVOR

Six weeks ago, you opened this workbook.

Today, you're not the same person.

You've done the hard work of examining your heart—your Moabs, your bitterness, your unforgiveness. You've learned that forgiveness isn't forgetting; it's choosing not to let the offense define you anymore. You've taken your first step into the field.

Ruth arrived in Bethlehem empty-handed but not empty-hearted. She had made her choice. She had clung to the right thing. And favor was waiting.

So is yours.

But here's what I want you to remember: this isn't graduation. It's a beginning. The work you've done in these six sessions? It's not a box to check off—it's a foundation to build on. Forgiveness may need to be chosen again tomorrow. Obedience will be tested next week. The journey of becoming the person God created you to be is lifelong.

And that's okay. Because His *chesed* never stops.

A Prayer for You

Lord, thank You for this person. They showed up. They did the work. They let You into the hard places.

Now I ask You to guard what You've planted. Don't let the enemy steal the seeds of freedom. When old thoughts try to creep back, remind them to change the channel. When they're tempted to pick up what they've laid down, give them the strength to leave it at Your feet.

They are not dis-appointed from their destiny—they're walking straight toward it.

We're waiting for our seventh measure. We're trusting in Your chesed that never stops. We're believing that You'll complete what You've begun.

And until then, we rest in this: "Being confident of this very thing, that He who has begun a good work in you will complete it until the day of Jesus Christ." (Philippians 1:6)

In Jesus' name, Amen.

— Melinda

STUDY TWO

FROM RISK TO REDEMPTION

Seven Sessions on Stepping Into Your Destiny

"What I am doing you do not understand now, but afterward you will understand." — John 13:7

SESSION SEVEN
WHEN GOD NOTICES YOU

Receiving Grace You Don't Deserve

Ruth 2:8-16

OPENING PRAYER

Begin with prayer, asking God to open your heart to His Word.

ICEBREAKER

"Describe a time when someone showed you unexpected kindness."

____

____

____

WORD STUDY

CHESED (חֶסֶד)

H2617 KHEH-sed

Meaning: steadfast love, covenant faithfulness, unfailing kindness

THE word of Ruth. *Chesed* appears three times in this small book (1:8, 2:20, 3:10), and it's the theological heartbeat of the entire story. God's *chesed* pursues when you run, provides when you doubt, stays when others leave, works when you can't see it, and never stops. Every session from here forward builds on this foundation.

TEACHING: Grace Beyond Deserving

"Her hap was to light on a part of the field belonging unto Boaz." The Hebrew suggests something that appears to be chance but is actually divine providence. Ruth didn't know whose field she entered. She was just looking for someone who would let her glean. But God was orchestrating every step.

Boaz noticed her immediately. "Whose damsel is this?" When he learned she was the Moabitess who had returned with Naomi, he did something extraordinary: he invited her to stay in his field, drink from his water, eat at his table, and glean among the sheaves—not just behind the reapers, but right alongside them. Then he instructed his workers to deliberately leave extra grain for her.

This is *chesed*—lovingkindness that goes beyond obligation. Boaz owed Ruth nothing. The Law required him to let her glean the leftovers, but nothing more. Yet he poured out favor she hadn't earned and couldn't repay. Ruth's response? "Why have I found grace in thine eyes, that thou shouldest take knowledge of me, seeing I am a stranger?" She knew she didn't deserve this. That's exactly the point. *Chesed* isn't about deserving. It's about a generous giver who delights in giving to those who have nothing to offer in return.

Boaz's blessing in Ruth 2:12 reveals his spiritual discernment: "The LORD recompense thy work, and a full reward be given thee of the LORD God of Israel, under whose wings thou art come to trust." The Hebrew word for "wings" is *kanaph*, which can also mean the corner or edge of a garment. This same word will appear again when Ruth asks Boaz to spread his "skirt" (*kanaph*) over her in chapter 3. Boaz prayed that God would cover Ruth with His wings; later, Ruth would ask Boaz to be the answer to his own prayer. Sometimes God uses us to fulfill the very prayers we pray for others.

Notice how Boaz's generosity escalated throughout chapter 2. First, he gave her permission to stay in his field (v. 8). Then protection among his workers (v. 9). Then access to water his servants had drawn (v. 9). Then a personal invitation to share his meal (v. 14). Then secret instructions to his workers to leave extra grain for her (v. 16). Each gift exceeded the previous one. This is how God often works—testing our faithfulness with smaller gifts before entrusting larger ones. Ruth's humble gratitude at each level opened the door to the next level of blessing.

Ruth's response to grace is instructive: "Let me find favour in thy sight, my lord; for that thou hast comforted me, and for that thou hast spoken friendly unto thine handmaid, though I be not like unto one of thine handmaidens" (v. 13). She received the gift without false humility ("Oh, I couldn't possibly accept this") or entitled expectation ("Well, it's about time someone helped me"). She acknowledged what she received, expressed genuine gratitude, and recognized she didn't deserve it. This is how we should receive God's grace—neither refusing it nor demanding it, but humbly accepting what we could never earn.

KEY THEMES
- God sees you when you feel invisible
- Grace is favor we don't deserve
- Character precedes blessing
- *Chesed* never stops

DISCUSSION QUESTIONS
1. What had Boaz heard about Ruth?

____

____

____

2. Do you struggle to receive grace you feel you don't deserve?

3. What does Boaz's kindness reveal about God's character?

4. Who has been a 'Boaz' in your life?

PERSONAL REFLECTION

• *Do I see myself as worthy of grace?*

• *What 'report' would others give about my character?*

• *Where might God's chesed be working that I'm missing?*

APPLICATION CHALLENGE

This week: BE a Boaz for someone this week. Also practice receiving grace without minimizing it.

CLOSING PRAYER

"Lord, thank You for seeing me. Help me receive Your grace and extend it to others. Amen."

MEMORY VERSE

"Why have I found grace in thine eyes, seeing I am a stranger? — Ruth 2:10"

NOTES

SESSION EIGHT

OBEDIENCE THAT DOESN'T MAKE SENSE

Trusting When You Don't Understand

Ruth 3:1-5 • John 13:1-17

OPENING PRAYER

Begin with prayer, asking God to open your heart to His Word.

ICEBREAKER

"Has God ever asked you to do something that didn't make sense at the time?"

____

____

____

WORD STUDY

MANOACH (מָנוֹחַ)

H4494 mah-NO-akh

Meaning: rest, a resting place, security (Ruth 1:9; 3:1)

Naomi sought 'rest' for Ruth—not just physical rest, but the security of being under a husband's covering and protection. This rest required Ruth to take an enormous risk.

TEACHING: Trusting Risky Counsel

Naomi's instructions to Ruth must have seemed outrageous: "Wash thyself, and anoint thee, and put thy raiment upon thee, and get thee down to the floor: but make not thyself known unto the man, until he shall have done eating and drinking... uncover his feet, and lay thee down."

This was a proposal of marriage according to ancient Near Eastern custom, but it was also a scandalous risk. Ruth was a foreign widow approaching a wealthy landowner in the middle of the night at a threshing floor—a place known for drinking and celebration. If Boaz misunderstood her intentions or rejected her approach, her reputation would be destroyed. If anyone saw her, the gossip would ruin both of them.

Yet Ruth's response demonstrates complete trust: "All that thou sayest unto me I will do." She didn't argue. She didn't ask for a safer plan. She didn't demand that God provide a less vulnerable path to provision. Sometimes obedience requires us to trust counsel that doesn't make sense to us, to take risks that feel dangerous, to position ourselves in ways that require complete dependence on God's protection. Ruth went to that threshing floor not knowing how Boaz would respond—but knowing she had obeyed.

The threshing floor was a significant location in Scripture. It was where grain was separated from chaff—where what was valuable was distinguished from what was worthless. Gideon met the angel of the Lord at a threshing floor (Judges 6:11). David purchased Araunah's threshing floor, which became the site of Solomon's temple (2 Samuel 24:18-25). Threshing floors were places of divine encounter and covenant transaction. Ruth wasn't just approaching a man; she was approaching a place where destinies were decided, where God had historically revealed Himself, where the valuable was separated from the worthless.

Naomi's instructions included preparation: "Wash thyself, and anoint thee, and put thy raiment upon thee." Ruth was to remove the garments of her widowhood and present herself as available for marriage. This required her to publicly declare that her season of mourning was complete—a vulnerable statement that invited scrutiny and judgment. Some in Bethlehem might have thought it too soon. Others might have questioned a Moabitess presuming to marry an Israelite. Ruth had to be willing to endure the opinions of others to pursue the destiny God had for her. What preparation is God asking of you that requires you to publicly declare a change in season?

Consider the faith required to uncover Boaz's feet and lie down. Ruth was placing herself in a position of complete vulnerability—she would have no defense if Boaz chose to take advantage of her, no excuse if others discovered her there, no recourse if he rejected her proposal. She was betting everything on his character. This is ultimately what faith requires: positioning ourselves vulnerably before God and trusting His character when we have no control over the outcome. Are you willing to put yourself in a position where only God's faithfulness can protect you?

KEY THEMES
- We don't need to understand to obey
- Trusting our own understanding can dishonor God
- 'Afterward you will understand'
- Obedience is the proof of trust

DISCUSSION QUESTIONS
1. Ruth obeyed without fully understanding. What made that possible?

____

____

____

2. How do we sometimes dishonor God while thinking we're being faithful?

____

____

____

3. Which biblical example (Abraham, Joseph, Moses) resonates with your situation?

____

____

____

4. What is God asking you to do that doesn't make sense?

____

____

____

PERSONAL REFLECTION

• *Where am I trusting my own understanding instead of God's Word?*

____

____

____

• *What godly counsel have I resisted because it seemed risky?*

____

____

____

• *Can I say 'All that You say, I will do'?*

____

____

____

APPLICATION CHALLENGE

This week: Identify one area where God seems to be asking you to obey without full understanding. Write John 13:7 on a card and read it daily.

____

____

____

____

CLOSING PRAYER

"Lord, help me say with Ruth, 'All that You say, I will do.' I trust that afterward I will understand. Amen."

MEMORY VERSE

"What I am doing you do not understand now, but afterward you will understand. — John 13:7"

NOTES

SESSION NINE

THE RISK OF VULNERABILITY

Asking For What You Need

Ruth 3:6-9

OPENING PRAYER

Begin with prayer, asking God to open your heart to His Word.

ICEBREAKER

"What's hardest for you to ask for—help, forgiveness, or something you want?"

WORD STUDY

GOEL (גָּאַל)

H1350 go-EL

Meaning kinsman-redeemer

A close relative responsible for protecting vulnerable family members, redeeming property that had been sold, avenging wrongs, and preserving the family name. The role required both relationship (you had to be kin) and resources (you had to be able to pay). Jesus is our ultimate Goel—He became our kinsman through the incarnation and paid our redemption price with His blood.

KANAPH (כָּנָף)

H3671 kah-NAHF

Meaning wing, corner, edge of a garment

The same word used for God's protective "wings" in Ruth 2:12 and the "skirt" Ruth asked Boaz to spread over her. It symbolizes covering, protection, and covenant relationship.

TEACHING: Holy Vulnerability

"Spread thy skirt over thine handmaid; for thou art a near kinsman." With these words, Ruth asked Boaz to redeem her.

This took enormous courage. Ruth was asking for what she needed, clearly and directly. She wasn't hinting or hoping Boaz would figure it out. She wasn't passive, waiting for him to make the first move. She positioned herself, spoke plainly, and trusted him with her vulnerability.

Ruth's request used powerful symbolism. The Hebrew word *kanaph* means wing, corner, or edge of a garment—the same word Boaz used when he prayed that Ruth would find refuge under God's "wings" (Ruth 2:12). Ruth was essentially asking Boaz to be God's answer to his own prayer—to extend the protective covering over her that he had asked God to provide. Sometimes we are meant to be the answers to our own prayers, to put feet to the blessings we've spoken over others.

The spreading of a garment over someone was a recognized proposal of marriage in ancient Near Eastern culture. We see this symbolism in Ezekiel 16:8, where God describes His covenant relationship with Israel: "I spread my skirt over thee, and covered thy nakedness... and thou becamest mine." Ruth wasn't being seductive; she was invoking a culturally appropriate proposal that carried deep theological significance. She was asking to be covered, protected, and brought into covenant relationship—a picture of what Christ does for His bride, the Church.

Ruth identified Boaz as a *go'el*—a kinsman-redeemer. She recognized that Boaz was both willing and able to redeem what had been lost.

Many of us struggle to ask for what we need—from God or from others. We hint. We hope. We wait. We assume people should know. But Ruth teaches us that there's a time to take holy risks, to make ourselves vulnerable, to ask directly for redemption. Boaz's response to Ruth's vulnerability? "Blessed be thou of the LORD, my daughter... thou hast shewed more kindness in the latter end than at the beginning." He honored her courage. Your Kinsman-Redeemer will honor yours too.

The act of uncovering Boaz's feet was deeply symbolic. In ancient Near Eastern culture, a servant would lie at their master's feet. Ruth was positioning herself as a servant, acknowledging Boaz's authority and her dependence on his decision. But she was also proposing marriage by asking him to spread his garment over her—a symbolic covering that represented protection, provision, and covenant. Ruth combined humility and boldness in a single act: she knew her place, but she also knew what she was asking for.

Notice Ruth identified herself specifically: "I am Ruth thine handmaid." In the darkness, Boaz couldn't see her face clearly. She could have remained anonymous, could have let mystery work in her favor. Instead, she named herself—including all the baggage that name carried. She was Ruth the Moabitess, the foreigner, the widow of Mahlon. She didn't hide behind ambiguity or try to be someone she wasn't. True vulnerability requires us to show up as ourselves, not as the version we think others want to see.

Boaz's response reveals his character. He could have taken advantage of a vulnerable woman in the dark. Instead, he blessed her, protected her reputation, and committed to pursuing redemption through proper channels. Scripture introduces Boaz as "a mighty man of wealth" (Ruth 2:1), but here we see that his worth wasn't just about resources; it was about the nobility of his character. He called her "my daughter"—a term of tender care, not condescension. He honored her initiative rather than shaming her for her boldness. The character of the person you make yourself vulnerable to matters. Ruth had observed Boaz's integrity in the fields before trusting him at the threshing floor. Don't give your vulnerability to someone who hasn't earned it through consistent character over time.

KEY THEMES

- Redemption often requires vulnerability
- We must position ourselves and ask
- God's wings often come through human covering
- Jesus is our Kinsman-Redeemer

DISCUSSION QUESTIONS

1. What did Ruth risk at the threshing floor?

____

____

____

2. How do we expect God to provide without human instruments?

____

____

____

3. What 'threshing floor' moment might God be calling you to?

____

____

____

4. How does knowing Jesus is your Goel affect how you approach Him?

____

____

____

PERSONAL REFLECTION

• *What am I afraid to ask for?*

• *What redemption do I need that I haven't asked for?*

• *Where am I expecting God to act without positioning myself?*

• *Who are you pretending to be instead of showing up as yourself—and when did you start believing the real you wasn't enough?*

APPLICATION CHALLENGE

This week: Identify one thing you need to ask for. Take the risk. Ask.

CLOSING PRAYER

"Lord Jesus, You are my Goel. Give me courage to position myself and ask. Amen."

MEMORY VERSE

"Spread thy skirt over thine handmaid; for thou art a near kinsman. — Ruth 3:9"

NOTES

SESSION TEN

CHARACTER THAT OPENS DOORS

Becoming a Person of Valor

Ruth 3:10-15 • Proverbs 31:10

OPENING PRAYER

Begin with prayer, asking God to open your heart to His Word.

ICEBREAKER

"If someone watched your life for a month, how would they describe your character?"

WORD STUDY

ESHET CHAYIL (אֵשֶׁת חַיִל)

H802+H2428 EH-shet KHAH-yil

Meaning: person of valor; eshet chayil (woman of valor) and ish chayil (man of valor)

'All the city knows thou art a virtuous woman.' Ruth had no pedigree or wealth, yet everyone knew her character. How we live when nobody important is watching becomes who we are.

TEACHING: Becoming a Person of Valor

"All the city of my people doth know that thou art a virtuous woman." Boaz used the phrase eshet chayil—woman of valor—the same words that open Proverbs 31. But Ruth had no pedigree that would merit this title. She was a Moabitess, a foreigner, a widow who gleaned in fields for food. By every external measure, she was nobody.

Yet "all the city" knew her character. How? Because character is built in the ordinary, unseen moments and revealed when it matters. Every day Ruth went to the fields, she demonstrated faithfulness. Every evening she brought grain home to Naomi, she showed loyalty. Every interaction with the workers revealed her integrity. She didn't suddenly become virtuous at the threshing floor—she had been becoming virtuous all along.

Boaz called Ruth *eshet chayil* after her risky midnight visit. Her boldness didn't diminish her virtue; it demonstrated it. True virtue isn't timidity dressed up as modesty. It's courage, strength, and moral excellence that acts decisively when the moment requires it. The question isn't whether you have an impressive background. The question is: What would "all the city" say about your character based on how you live when no one important is watching?

The Hebrew word *chayil* appears over 240 times in Scripture. It's translated as army, wealth, strength, ability, and virtue depending on context. When applied to soldiers, it means mighty warriors. When applied to wealth, it means substantial resources. When applied to character, it means moral strength and excellence. This isn't passive goodness but active excellence, not mere innocence but proven integrity under pressure.

Notice that "all the city of my people" knew Ruth's character. Her reputation wasn't built in a day or through one grand gesture. It was established through consistent daily choices observed over time. The workers in the field saw how Ruth conducted herself. The community watched how she handled her poverty and widowhood. Boaz's workers saw how he treated the vulnerable—inviting a foreign widow to glean safely, providing extra grain, and protecting her from harassment. Character isn't what you do when everyone is watching—it's who you are when you think no one notices. But someone always notices, and reputation is built one observed moment at a time.

Remarkably, the book of Ruth gives us both the male and female forms of this word. Ruth is called *eshet chayil* (woman of valor) in Ruth 3:11, while Boaz is introduced as ish *gibbor chayil* (mighty man of valor) in Ruth 2:1. Boaz's *chayil* wasn't just about his wealth—it was proven in his character. He swore an oath invoking God's name (v. 13), protected Ruth's reputation by sending her home before dawn, acknowledged the complication of the nearer kinsman rather than hiding it, and committed to handle everything properly and publicly. Two people of integrity recognized each other's character and responded honorably. God brings people of *chayil* together—are you becoming someone a person of valor would recognize?

KEY THEMES
- Character is built in private, revealed in public
- Reputation precedes request
- *Eshet chayil* is about consistent integrity, not perfection
- Character opens doors that circumstances cannot

DISCUSSION QUESTIONS
1. How did 'all the city' know Ruth's character?

____

____

____

2. What's the difference between reputation and character?

____

____

____

3. Boaz called Ruth 'virtuous' AFTER her risky act. What does this tell us?

____

____

____

4. What character trait do you most want to be known for?

____

____

____

PERSONAL REFLECTION

• *What would 'all the city' say about my character?*

____

____

____

• *Where is there a gap between my public and private character?*

____

____

____

• *What daily choices am I making that build or erode character?*

____

____

____

APPLICATION CHALLENGE

This week: Choose one character trait to develop. Focus on it especially when no one is watching.

CLOSING PRAYER

"Lord, build my character in private so that when tests come, I'm ready. Amen."

MEMORY VERSES

"Who can find a virtuous woman? For her price is far above rubies." — Proverbs 31:10

"There was a mighty man of valour... and his name was Boaz." — Ruth 2:1

(Both verses use the Hebrew word chayil—strength, valor, excellence of character.)

NOTES

SESSION ELEVEN
THE DISCIPLINE OF WAITING

Trusting God's Timing
Ruth 3:16-18 • Isaiah 26:3

OPENING PRAYER

Begin with prayer, asking God to open your heart to His Word.

ICEBREAKER

"What's harder—taking a risk or waiting after you've taken the risk?"

____

____

____

WORD STUDY

YASHAB (יָשַׁב)

H3427 yah-SHAHV

Meaning: to sit, dwell, remain, stay

"Sit still" isn't passive resignation—it's active trust. While Ruth waited, Boaz worked. While you wait, God works.

SHALOM SHALOM (שָׁלוֹם שָׁלוֹם)

H7965 (doubled) shah-LOHM shah-LOHM

Meaning: perfect peace, complete wholeness

The doubling of *shalom* in Hebrew intensifies the meaning—not just peace, but perfect, complete, abiding peace. Isaiah 26:3 promises *shalom shalom* to those whose minds are fixed on Him in trust.

TEACHING: Active Waiting

"Sit still, my daughter, until thou know how the matter will fall." After all Ruth's initiative and risk, Naomi told her to wait. But *yashab*—to sit still—isn't passive resignation. It's active trust. It's the discipline of not interfering with what God is doing.

Naomi understood something crucial: "The man will not be in rest, until he have finished the thing this day." While Ruth sat still, Boaz was working. While she waited at home, he was at the city gate handling legal proceedings, confronting the nearer kinsman, and securing the redemption. Her waiting wasn't wasted time—it was the space Boaz needed to complete what he had promised.

Ruth came home with six measures of barley—evidence of Boaz's commitment, provision for the waiting. This is how God works. He gives us evidence to sustain us while He completes what He's doing behind the scenes. Isaiah 26:3 promises "perfect peace"—shalom shalom—to the one whose mind is stayed on the Lord. The double repetition emphasizes completeness. Not anxious peace. Not partial peace. Perfect peace for those who trust Him enough to sit still while He works.

The six measures of barley Ruth carried home were significant. Six is the number of man, of incompleteness, of work before rest. Seven represents completion and Sabbath. Boaz gave Ruth six measures as a promise that the seventh—the completion—was coming. It was tangible evidence that redemption was in process even though it wasn't finished yet. When we're in the waiting, God often gives us "six measures"—evidence of His commitment, provision for the journey, assurance that the seventh measure is on its way.

Naomi's wisdom in verse 18 is remarkable: "Sit still, my daughter, until thou know how the matter will fall: for the man will not be in rest, until he have finished the thing this day." She understood Boaz's character. She knew he wouldn't delay or forget. The Hebrew word for "rest" here (*shaqat*) means to be quiet, settled, or at peace. Boaz's integrity meant he would have no inner rest until he fulfilled his promise. When God gives you a promise through a person of character, you can trust they will not rest until it's complete.

There's a profound application here for our relationship with Christ. He is our Kinsman-Redeemer who will not rest until He has finished the work of redemption. Philippians 1:6 promises that "he which hath begun a good work in you will perform it until the day of Jesus Christ." We can sit still in confident peace because our Redeemer is actively working on our behalf. The question isn't whether He will finish; it's whether we will trust Him enough to rest while He does.

KEY THEMES
- 'Sit still' is active trust, not passive resignation
- While we wait, God works
- Shalom shalom—perfect peace for those who trust
- Evidence during waiting sustains us

DISCUSSION QUESTIONS

1. Ruth came home with six measures—evidence. What evidence do you have of God's work?

2. 'Sit still' is not 'do nothing.' What's the difference?

3. What do you typically do instead of waiting?

4. What matter do you need to wait on to see 'how it will fall'?

PERSONAL REFLECTION

• *Am I trying to control outcomes only God can handle?*

• *What does 'sitting still' look like in my situation?*

• *List my 'six measures'—evidence of God's faithfulness:*

APPLICATION CHALLENGE

This week: Practice 'sitting still.' Identify one situation you've been trying to control and release it to God.

____

____

____

CLOSING PRAYER

"Lord, teach me to sit still. Give me shalom shalom. You will not rest until You've finished. Amen."

MEMORY VERSE

"Thou wilt keep him in perfect peace, whose mind is stayed on thee. — Isaiah 26:3"

NOTES

SESSION TWELVE
THE COST OF REDEMPTION
True Redemption Requires Sacrifice
Ruth 4:1-12

OPENING PRAYER

Begin with prayer, asking God to open your heart to His Word.

ICEBREAKER

"Has anyone ever 'redeemed' something for you—paid a price they didn't have to pay?"

____

____

____

WORD STUDY

QANAH (קָנָה)

H7069 kah-NAH

Meaning: to acquire, buy, purchase, redeem

The nearer kinsman would redeem land but NOT Ruth—protecting himself. Boaz paid full price, took full responsibility, declared publicly. True redemption requires sacrifice, not sentiment.

TEACHING: The Price of Redemption

Boaz went to the city gate where legal business was conducted. There was a nearer kinsman who had first right of redemption. When Boaz offered him the opportunity to redeem Naomi's land, the man agreed—until he learned Ruth was part of the package. "I cannot redeem it for myself, lest I mar mine own inheritance."

The nearer kinsman was willing to acquire property but not responsibility. He would take the land but not the Moabite widow who came with it. Redemption that required personal cost? That might affect his own estate? He passed. But Boaz declared publicly, "I have bought all that was Elimelech's... Moreover Ruth the Moabitess... have I purchased to be my wife."

This is the difference between convenient religion and costly redemption. The nearer kinsman represents everyone who wants blessing without sacrifice, inheritance without investment, redemption without relationship. But true redemption always costs the redeemer. Boaz paid full price for everything —land, legacy, and the foreign widow everyone else rejected. This is how Jesus redeems us. He doesn't redeem the acceptable parts and leave the rest. He purchases all of us—including the parts others wouldn't touch—and declares publicly that we are His.

The Hebrew word for redeemer is *go'el*. A *go'el* was a close relative who had both the right and the resources to redeem what had been lost. The *go'el* could buy back family land that had been sold due to poverty (Leviticus 25:25), redeem a family member sold into slavery (Leviticus 25:47-49), avenge the blood of a murdered relative (Numbers 35:19), and marry a deceased relative's widow to continue the family line (Deuteronomy 25:5-6). Boaz fulfilled this role completely for Ruth and Naomi, becoming a living picture of what Jesus does for us.

The nearer kinsman's refusal reveals a critical truth: being able to redeem isn't the same as being willing to redeem. The nearer kinsman had the legal right but lacked the heart. He calculated the cost and decided Ruth wasn't worth it. His words—"lest I mar mine own inheritance"—showed his priority was protecting himself rather than restoring others. True redemption requires a redeemer who values the person above the price. Jesus could have calculated the cost of our redemption and decided we weren't worth it. Instead, He looked at us and said, "I purchase all."

The transaction happened at the city gate in front of ten elders—witnesses who made the redemption legally binding and publicly known. Boaz didn't redeem Ruth secretly. He declared his intentions before the community, accepting responsibility openly and permanently. When Jesus redeemed us, He did it publicly on a cross, visible to all, with witnesses who recorded it for generations. Our redemption isn't a private arrangement or secret deal. It's a public declaration that we belong to Him, that He paid the price, that we are His purchased possession forever.

KEY THEMES
- Redemption always costs the redeemer
- The nearer kinsman wasn't willing to pay full price
- Boaz redeemed publicly, completely, without hesitation
- Jesus paid what no one else would pay

DISCUSSION QUESTIONS
1. Why wouldn't the nearer kinsman redeem Ruth?

____

____

____

2. What was Boaz willing to do that he wasn't?

____

____

____

3. Why does public declaration matter?

____

____

____

4. What has Jesus been willing to 'purchase' that others wouldn't touch?

____

____

____

PERSONAL REFLECTION

• *Have I accepted that Jesus redeemed ALL of me—even parts others reject?*

____

____

____

• *Is there an area I'm treating as 'unredeemable'?*

____

____

____

• *Who might God be calling me to help redeem?*

____

____

____

APPLICATION CHALLENGE

This week: Meditate on what Jesus paid to redeem you. Write a prayer of gratitude.

____

____

____

____

____

CLOSING PRAYER

"Lord Jesus, You paid the price no one else would pay. Help me live as someone fully redeemed. Amen."

MEMORY VERSE

"Ye were not redeemed with corruptible things, as silver and gold... but with the precious blood of Christ."

— 1 Peter 1:18-19

NOTES

SESSION THIRTEEN
YOUR STORY IN HIS STORY

Legacy, Destiny, Purpose Fulfilled
Ruth 4:13-22 • Philippians 2:13

OPENING PRAYER

Begin with prayer, asking God to open your heart to His Word.

ICEBREAKER

"What has been the most meaningful truth you've discovered in this study?"

____

____

____

WORD STUDY
Philippians 2:12-13

ENERGEO (ἐνεργέω) G1754 en-erg-EH-oh

Meaning: To be operative, to be at work, to produce effects. This is God working IN you—supplying the power, the desire, and the ability. You don't generate the energy; He does. Your job is to cooperate with what He's already doing inside you.

KATERGAZOMAI (κατεργάζομαι) G2716 kat-erg-AD-zom-ahee

Meaning: To perform, accomplish, achieve, work out to completion. This is what YOU do—actively working out what God is working in. The prefix "kata" intensifies the action, meaning to work something all the way through to its finish. God supplies the power (*energeo*); you supply the participation (*katergazomai*).

Naomi went from 'Mara' to holding her grandson. Ruth became an ancestor of Jesus. God transforms Mara back to Naomi—He can do the same for you. Your story is part of His bigger story.

TEACHING: Your Story in His Story

"So Boaz took Ruth, and she was his wife... and she bare a son." The women of Bethlehem celebrated with Naomi: "Blessed be the LORD, which hath not left thee this day without a kinsman." The woman who called herself Mara—bitter—now held a grandson. The woman who said she returned "empty" was now full beyond measure.

But the story doesn't end with personal blessing. The genealogy that closes the book reveals the larger purpose: "And Obed begat Jesse, and Jesse begat David." Ruth the Moabitess—the foreigner, the outsider, the woman from the forbidden nation—became the great-grandmother of King David and an ancestor of Jesus Christ.

This is what God does with yielded lives. Your story isn't just about your redemption. It's about what God will do through your redemption for generations you'll never meet. Ruth didn't know she was positioning herself in the lineage of the Messiah. She was simply being faithful—one day at a time, one choice at a time. That's all any of us can do. Your obedience today is writing a story that won't be fully told until eternity. Trust the Author.

The women of Bethlehem's blessing over Naomi reveals a beautiful transformation: "Blessed be the LORD, which hath not left thee this day without a kinsman, that his name may be famous in Israel. And he shall be unto thee a restorer of thy life, and a nourisher of thine old age." The word "restorer" (shuwb) is the same root word used for repentance and return. God had brought Naomi back—not just to Bethlehem, but back to life, back to hope, back to identity. The woman who called herself bitter was being made pleasant again.

Notice what the women said about Ruth: *"Thy daughter-in-law, which loveth thee, which is better to thee than seven sons."* In a culture where sons were the ultimate blessing, this was an extraordinary statement. Seven sons would have been considered a complete family blessing. Yet Ruth—a foreign daughter-in-law—was declared better than seven sons. God doesn't just restore what was lost; He gives more than we had before. Naomi lost two sons in Moab but gained a daughter-in-law worth more than seven. Our Redeemer doesn't just bring us back to where we were; He takes us further than we could have gone without the loss.

Ruth appears in Matthew's genealogy of Jesus (Matthew 1:5)—one of only five women mentioned in the entire lineage. Each of these women had an unusual or scandalous story: Tamar, Rahab, Ruth, Bathsheba, and Mary. God deliberately included the outsiders, the broken, and the unexpected in Jesus' family line. If you think your background disqualifies you from being used by God, remember that a Moabite widow who gleaned in fields became an ancestor of the Messiah. God doesn't just tolerate our broken stories; He writes them into His redemptive narrative. Your story isn't a footnote—it's part of the text.

KEY THEMES

- Redemption produces life and legacy
- Naomi's transformation: from Mara back to blessed
- Your story is part of a bigger story
- God is working in you to fulfill His purpose

DISCUSSION QUESTIONS

1. How does God restore what we thought was lost forever?

2. How might your pain be part of a bigger story you can't see?

3. What has this study taught you about God's chesed?

4. Where are you in your Ruth journey now?

PERSONAL REFLECTION

- *How has my understanding of redemption changed?*

• *What legacy might come from my season of restoration?*

____

____

____

• *How can I be part of someone else's redemption story?*

____

____

____

APPLICATION CHALLENGE

This week: Write your own 'Ruth story.' Consider sharing it with someone who needs hope.

____

____

____

____

CLOSING PRAYER

"Lord, complete the redemption You've begun. Use my journey to bring hope to others. Amen."

MEMORY VERSE

"For it is God which worketh in you both to will and to do of his good pleasure. — Philippians 2:13"

NOTES

STUDY TWO CONCLUSION: REDEMPTION REALIZED

Redemption realized.

Not because your life is perfect now. Not because every question has been answered. But because you've walked the journey and let God do His work.

You're not the person who started this study. You've released what was holding you back. You've stepped into what was waiting for you. You've learned that God's timing is worth trusting, even when the waiting feels endless.

Ruth went from foreign widow to ancestor of Christ. Not because she was perfect, but because she was faithful. One step at a time. One choice at a time. One day at a time.

That's your path too.

Boaz sent Ruth home with six measures of barley—provision for the waiting, evidence of his commitment, a promise of what was to come. But the seventh measure? That was the completion. The redemption. The fulfillment of everything she'd hoped for.

You've received your six measures through this study. You've been given truth, tools, and transformation. But the seventh measure is still coming. God isn't finished with you yet. The work continues—not because you failed, but because redemption is a lifelong journey.

Keep gleaning. Keep trusting. Keep becoming.

A Prayer for You

Lord Jesus, my Kinsman-Redeemer, thank You for this person. You saw them when they felt invisible. You pursued them when they wandered. You redeemed what they thought was lost forever.

Now use them. Let their story bring hope to someone else walking through famine. Let their forgiveness unlock someone else's chains. Let their faithfulness be the example another person needs to take their own first step.

We're waiting for our seventh measure. We're trusting in Your chesed that never stops. We're believing that You'll complete what You've begun.

And until then, we rest in this: "Being confident of this very thing, that He who has begun a good work in you will complete it until the day of Jesus Christ." (Philippians 1:6)

Their chesed journey doesn't end here—it multiplies. In Your name, Amen.

— Melinda

APPENDIX A: HEBREW WORD GLOSSARY

BATACH (בָּטַח) H982 baw-TAKH — to trust, have confidence in; deep security in God's character

CHESED (חֶסֶד) H2617 KHEH-sed — lovingkindness, unfailing love, loyal love, mercy; covenant love that goes beyond obligation

DABAQ (דָּבַק) H1692 daw-BAK — to cling, cleave, hold fast; the same word used for marriage in Genesis 2:24

ESHET CHAYIL (אֵשֶׁת חַיִל) H802+H2428 EH-shet KHAH-yil — woman of valor, virtuous woman; the male equivalent is ish chayil (man of valor). Both describe strength, moral excellence, and proven character. Ruth 3:11, Ruth 2:1

GALAL (גָּלַל) H1556 gaw-LAL — to roll, commit; rolling yourself onto God

GOEL (גֹּאֵל) H1350 go-EL — kinsman-redeemer; one responsible for protecting family interests

KANAPH (כָּנָף) H3671 kah-NAHF — wing, corner, edge of a garment; symbolizes covering, protection, and covenant relationship (Ruth 2:12; 3:9)

LAQAT (לָקַט) H3950 law-KAT — to glean, gather, pick up; gathering what others have left behind

MANOACH (מָנוֹחַ) H4494 maw-NO-akh — rest, a resting place, security

MARA (מָרָא) H4755 MAW-raw — bitter, bitterness

NASA (נָשָׂא) H5375 naw-SAW — to lift, carry away; picturing forgiveness as removing a burden

PAQAD (פָּקַד) H6485 paw-KAD — to visit, attend to, care for; God taking intentional action

QANAH (קָנָה) H7069 kaw-NAW — to acquire, buy, purchase, redeem

SALACH (סָלַח) H5545 saw-LAKH — to forgive, pardon; used exclusively of God's forgiveness

SHALOM (שָׁלוֹם) H7965 shaw-LOME — peace, completeness, wholeness; doubled shalom shalom = perfect peace

YASHAB (יָשַׁב) H3427 yaw-SHAB — to sit still, remain, dwell; active trust, not passive resignation

YASHAR (יָשָׁר) H3477 yaw-SHAR — straight, upright, pleasing, right

APPENDIX B: GREEK WORD GLOSSARY

AGAPE (ἀγάπη) G26 ah-GAH-pay — unconditional love; selfless, sacrificial love

APHIEMI (ἀφίημι) G863 af-EE-ay-mee — to send away, release, forgive; letting go of a debt or offense

CHARIS (χάρις) G5485 KHAR-ees — grace, favor; unmerited kindness

EIRENE (εἰρήνη) G1515 ay-RAY-nay — peace; equivalent to Hebrew shalom

ENERGEO (ἐνεργέω) G1754 en-erg-EH-oh — to be operative, be at work; God working IN you

KATERGAZOMAI (κατεργάζομαι) G2716 kat-erg-AD-zom-ahee — to perform, accomplish, work out to completion

MNAOMAI (μνάομαι) G3415 MNAH-oh-my — to remind, recall; God chooses NOT to bring up our sins

PISTIS (πίστις) G4102 PIS-tis — faith, trust, belief; confident assurance

APPENDIX C: MAP & TIMELINE

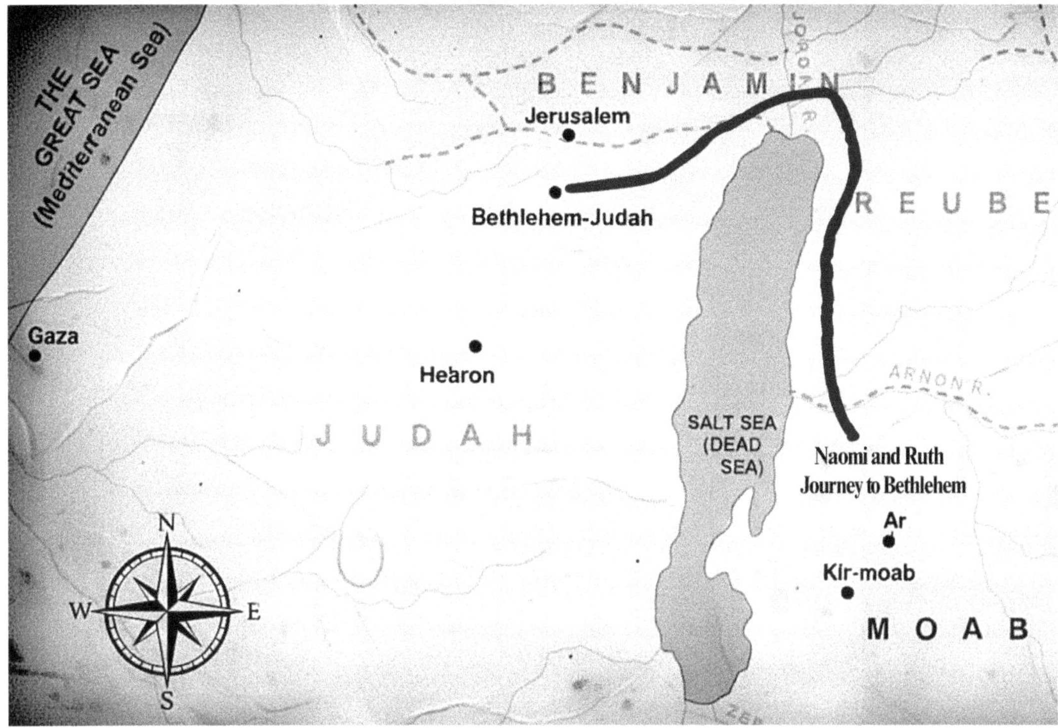

The Journey from Moab to Bethlehem: A Survival Timeline

Route Overview

- **Estimated Total Distance:** ~76 Miles (122 km)
- **Route Taken:** The Northern Route (Moab Plateau → Jordan Valley → Jericho → Judean Wilderness → Bethlehem)
- Estimated Duration: 10 Days
- **Elevation Change:** A total vertical climb of 3,300 feet in the final 48 hours.

TIMELINE:Day-by-Day Itinerary & Survival Risks

Days	Stage & Milestone	Terrain & Environment	Primary Dangers
1–2	**Departure:** Leaving Moab	Descending from the high Moabite plateau (3,000 ft elevation).	**Exposure:** High risk of dehydration as they leave the fertile plateau for arid canyons.
3–5	**The Valley:** Plains of Moab	Flat, dusty, and punishingly hot land approaching the Jordan River.	**Extreme Heat:** Temperatures often exceed 100°F. Risk of heatstroke and encounters with wild boars.
6	**The Crossing:** Jordan River	Crossing at the shallow "Fords of the Jordan" near Beth-nimrah.	**Drowning & Predators:** Strong currents could sweep travelers away. The thickets (The *Zor*) were home to lions and bears.
7–9	**The Ascent:** Judean Wilderness	A grueling climb from 800 ft *below* sea level to 2,500 ft *above*.	**Bandits:** The "Jericho Road" was notorious for bandits hiding in caves. Physical exhaustion from the steep 3,300 ft climb.
10	**Arrival:** Bethlehem	Entering the city gates as the barley harvest begins.	**Social Rejection:** Potential hostility or xenophobia toward Ruth as a Moabite foreigner.

APPENDIX D: THE GENTILES IN THE LINEAGE OF CHRIST

From Ruth to Jesus (Matthew 1:5-16)

Ruth is one of only four women in Matthew's genealogy of Jesus. All four were Gentiles or connected to Gentiles:

The Gentile Women
- TAMAR — Canaanite who posed as a prostitute to secure her place in the lineage (Genesis 38)
- RAHAB — Canaanite prostitute from Jericho who hid the spies (Joshua 2)
- RUTH — Moabitess, a widow from a forbidden nation who chose covenant with God (Book of Ruth)
- BATHSHEBA — wife of Uriah the Hittite, likely Hittite herself (2 Samuel 11)

The Men with Gentile Heritage
Because these Gentile women married into the line, their sons carried mixed heritage forward:
- PEREZ — son of Judah and Tamar, half-Canaanite (Genesis 38:29)
- BOAZ — son of Salmon and Rahab, half-Canaanite; the *ish chayil* who redeemed Ruth (Ruth 2:1)
- OBED — son of Boaz and Ruth, mixed Israelite/Canaanite/Moabite heritage (Ruth 4:17)
- JESSE — carried that same mixed lineage forward (Ruth 4:22)
- DAVID — the great king, great-grandson of Ruth the Moabitess (Ruth 4:22; Matthew 1:6)

The Theological Significance
Jesus didn't just come FOR the Gentiles—He came FROM them. The Messiah's bloodline was never "pure" by human standards. God intentionally wove outsiders, foreigners, and the unexpected into the very DNA of the Savior. This makes the gospel relevant to everyone—male or female, Jew or Gentile, insider or outsider. We are all part of God's redemption story.

A Note on the Two Genealogies
Some may ask: since Jesus was born of a virgin, His physical blood came through Mary alone. Joseph was His legal father, not His biological father. So does the Gentile heritage still apply?

Yes. Matthew 1 traces Jesus' legal lineage through Joseph, giving Him the legal right to David's throne. But Luke 3:23-38 is believed to trace Mary's lineage—and it also goes back through David. If Mary descended from David (through Nathan rather than Solomon), she carried that same heritage forward from Ruth, Boaz, Obed, and Jesse.

Either way, the point stands: Ruth the Moabitess is the great-grandmother of David, and David is an ancestor of both Joseph and Mary. Whether legally or biologically, God wove the outsiders into the Messiah's story.

No matter your lineage, your past, or your mistakes—

God's redemption reaches everyone. No one is too far outside.

APPENDIX E: FOR THOSE IN CRISIS

If you're in crisis right now, please know: Your pain is real. Asking for help is strength. You don't have to walk through this alone.

IMMEDIATE HELP

If you are in immediate danger, please call 911.

National Domestic Violence Hotline: 1-800-799-7233
Suicide Prevention Lifeline: 988
Crisis Text Line: Text HOME to 741741
Focus on the Family: 1-855-771-HELP (4357)
Need Him Global: chataboutjesus.com
GriefShare: griefshare.org

ADDICTION AND RECOVERY

SAMHSA National Helpline: 1-800-662-4357 (free, confidential, 24/7)
Celebrate Recovery: celebraterecovery.com

SEXUAL ASSAULT

RAINN (Rape, Abuse & Incest National Network): 1-800-656-4673 or rainn.org

MENTAL HEALTH

National Alliance on Mental Illness (NAMI): 1-800-950-6264
Men's Resource Center: mensresourcecenter.org

FINANCIAL CRISIS

211: Dial 2-1-1 for local resources (food, housing, utilities assistance)

FOR THOSE WHO'VE LOST A SPOUSE

Widow's Might Ministry: widowsmight.org
Modern Widows Club: modernwidowsclub.com

FOR THOSE WHO'VE LOST A CHILD

The Compassionate Friends: compassionatefriends.org

You are not alone. Help is available. God sees you.

APPENDIX F: LEADER'S GUIDE

Thank you for leading this study! Here are some guidelines:

• Prepare by reading the session and praying for your group

• Create a safe space for honest sharing

• Don't feel pressure to answer every question—let the Holy Spirit lead

• Allow silence, validate feelings and processing takes time

• Keep confidentiality

• Don't: Offer clichés, compare pain, push sharing, force forgiveness timelines.

• Do: Point participants to professional help when needed (see Appendix E)

SESSION-SPECIFIC GUIDANCE

Sessions 4-5 (Bitterness and Forgiveness): These sessions may cause deep wounds to surface. Have tissues available. Be prepared for tears, anger, or silence. The Forgiveness Inventory is a private exercise—never ask participants to share names aloud. If someone becomes visibly distressed, offer to speak privately after the session. Know your local counseling resources before these weeks.

Session 9 (Vulnerability): This session touches on themes of vulnerability and trust that may be sensitive for survivors of abuse or betrayal. In mixed-gender groups, be aware that discussions of Ruth's threshing floor encounter may prompt different reactions. Emphasize Boaz's protective response as the model of godly character. Never pressure anyone to share more than they're comfortable with.

For Mixed-Gender Groups: This study works beautifully for both men and women. Highlight how both Ruth (*eshet chayil*) and Boaz (*ish chayil*) model godly character. The Hebrew word *chayil* applies equally to both —Session 10 explores this fully. Encourage men to see themselves in Boaz's integrity, initiative, and protective leadership, while both men and women can learn from Ruth's faithfulness, courage, and vulnerability.

FLEXIBLE FORMATS

• Study One Only: 6 weeks • Study Two Only: 7 weeks (with brief recap of Study One) • Full Study: 13 weeks

SESSION SUGGESTED FORMAT (60-90 min)

Opening/Icebreaker: 10-15 min

Scripture: 5 min

Teaching: 15-20 min

Discussion: 20-25 min

Reflection: 10 min

Close: 5-10 min

MY STORY: JOURNALING PAGE

Use this page as a quick reference of what God has spoken to you through this study. Remember, "Your Story" one encounter at a time.

Until redemption is complete,

keep gleaning. Keep trusting.

Keep believing that His chesed hasn't stopped

and never will.

You are becoming the person God created you to be.